The Chapter of Kings
by
Mr Collins

*Exhibiting the most important events
in the English history*

a facsimile of the original edition

BODLEIAN LIBRARY
UNIVERSITY OF OXFORD

First published in 2005 by the Bodleian Library
Broad Street
Oxford
OX1 3BG

ISBN 1 85124 320 8

Designed by Dot Little
Printed and bound by Butler and Tanner, Frome, Somerset
A catalogue record for this book is available from the British Library

A facsimile from the Opie Collection of Children's Literature, Bodleian
Library, Opie D37

The
CHAPTER OF KINGS.

By
Mr. COLLINS.

MAGNA CHARTA.

LONDON.

Published Aug.ʳ 1, 1818, by J. Harris, Corner of St Pauls Church Yard.

CÆSAR invaded Britain about 53 years before Christ, and it remained subject to the Roman Power about 400 Years.

The Romans, in England, they once did sway,

The Saxons first came in the year 450, and remained 580 Years.

ALFRED in the Danish Camp.

And the Saxons, they after them, led the way,

EDMUND 2.nd surnamed Ironside endeavouring to terminate
the War by single combat with CANUTE the Dane.

And they tugg'd with the Danes, 'till an overthrow

The Battle of Hastings fought Oct.ʳ 14, 1066, in which King HAROLD was slain, and thus ended the Saxon Government.

They both of them got by the Norman Bow.

WILLIAM the CONQUEROR accepts the Crown 1066, and reigned 20 Years, 10 months, and 26 days.

Norman Willy, the Conqueror, long did reign.

WILLIAM RUFUS killed by an Arrow in the New Forest;
Aug.st 2.nd 1100.

Red Billy, his Son, by an Arrow was slain,

HENRY 1st for his learning was surnamed Beauclerc,
he built a Palace at Oxford, 1100 to 1135.

And Henry the First was a scholar bright,

STEPHEN at the Battle of Lincoln defended himself
'till his Battle-axe and Sword were both broken & he
was knocked down on his knees by a stone, 1135 to 1154.

Though Stephen was forc'd for his crown to fight,

HENRY 2nd reigned from 1154 to 1189 his plague was Arch bp
Becket; his consolation, Fair Rosamond.

Second Henry, Plantagenet's name did bear.

Published Augst 1 1818 by I Harris Corner of St P. l Ch. l Yd.

RICHARD 1st surnamed Cœur de Lion from 1189 to 1199.—he defeated SALADIN. and killed 40,000 of his Soldiers.

Richard, Cœur de Lion, was his Son and heir.

Magna-Charta was signed by KING JOHN, and the Barons
of England 1215.—he reigned from 1199 to 1216.

Famed Magna-Charta we gained from John,

HENRY 3rd from 1216 to 1272.—he agreed to conform to Magna
Charta and to hold three Parliaments annually.

Which Henry the Third put his seal upon.

EDWARD 1.st from 1272 to 1307.——he slew Llewellen the last of the Antient British Princes, and imprisoned John Baliol, King of the Scots, in the Tower.

His Son, Edward the First, was a Tiger bold,

EDWARD 2nd from 1307 to 1327.__he was conducted to the Tower on a miserable Horse by the rebels, and afterwards murdered in Berkley Castle.

Second Edward by rebels was bought and sold;

EDWARD 3.rd from 1327 to 1377.— celebrated not only for his conquests, but for supporting the dignity of the Crown, and the privileges of the people.

But Edward the Third was his subjects pride;

RICHARD 2ⁿᵈ from 1377 to 1399.— he resigned his Crown
and Kingdom, to Henry Duke of Lancaster.

His poor grandson, Richard, was popped aside.

HENRY 4th. from 1399 to 1413.—he commanded in person at the
Battle of Shrewsbury. with the PRINCE of WALES by his side.
who was wounded in the face by an Arrow.

Fourth Henry, of Lancaster, was a bold wight,

HENRY 5th from 1413 to 1422.— at the famous Battle of Agincourt, he defeated the French Army of 50,000 men with only 9000 of his own forces.

And his Son, the Fifth Henry, bravely did fight;

HENRY 6th from 1422 to 1461.— was imprisoned in the Tower by order of his Son Edward;— where he was murdered by Richard Duke of Gloster.

Sixth Henry, his Son, like a chick did pout.

EDWARD 4th from 1461 to 1483.— after the Battle of Towton..
he was Crown'd in the City of London, June 29, 1461.

When Fourth Edward, his cousin, had turned him out.

EDWARD 5th reigned two months and twelve days of
1483, and was smothered in the Tower, with his brother,
the Duke of York, by order of his Uncle Richard.

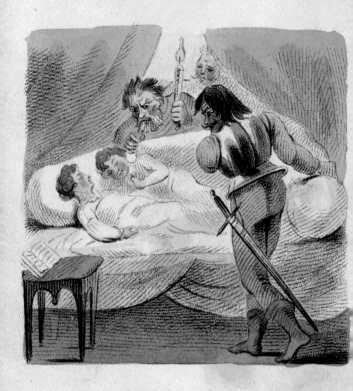

Poor Edward the Fifth, was young killed in his bed,

RICHARD 3rd from 1483 to 1485.—he was killed at the Battle of Bosworth-field, his body was thrown across a horse and interred at Leicester.

By his uncle, Richard, who was knocked on the head.

HENRY 7th from 1485 to 1509, who married the Princess Elizabeth
daughter of Edward 4th & thus united the houses of York and
Lancaster, — he established the Yeoman of the Guard.

By Henry the Seventh, who in fame grew big,

HENRY 8th from 1509 to 1547.—in his reign the Bible was translated into English,—towards the end of his life he was extremely corpulent.

And Henry the Eighth, who was fat as a pig.

EDWARD 6th from 1547 to 1553 was remarkable for his Virtue, Piety, and Humanity, he founded the Hospitals of Christ, St Thomas's, and Bridewell.

With Edward the Sixth we had tranquil days,

Published Augst 1st 1818 by J.Harris, Corner of St Pauls Church Yard.

MARY 1st from 1553 to 1558.—her reign was a continued scene of bloodshed, burning, and persecution, and her name was handed down by historians, as bloody Mary.

Though Mary, his Sister, made faggots to blaze;

ELIZABETH from 1558 to 1603.— she was Learned & Virtu-
ous, and selected such only to the Offices of Government
who were like herself; she exhorted her Army to protect
the Kingdom against the Spanish Armada.

But good Queen Bess was a glorious dame,

JAMES the 1st (of the House of Stuart) from 1603 to 1625.
he was pedantic, and wrote on Arbitrary Power, demon-
ology witchcraft &c.. the Gunpowder Plot was discovered
in his reign.

And King James the First from good Scotland came.

CHARLES 1st from 1625 to 1649.—he was a Prince of ele-
gant pursuits, but having too high a notion of the royal
prerogative, he became the victim of a furious party, &
was beheaded Jan.ry 30. 1649.

Charles the First was his son, and a martyr made

CHARLES 2nd from 1649, actually 1660 to 1685. his natural
disposition was affable and cheerful, and he affected
to be witty even to licentiousness.

Charles the Second, his son, was a comical blade ;

JAMES 2nd from 1685 to 1688._by his endeavours to overturn the Protestant Religion he lost the affection of his subjects,_he escaped from Rochester with his Son,& went to France, where he died in 1701.

James the Second, his brother, when hotly spurr'd,

WILLIAM the 3rd and MARY 2nd from 1688 to 1702. William at the Battle of the Boyne, defeated James, & his Allies on the 1st of July, 1690.

Ran away, I assure you, from William the Third.

ANNE from 1702 to 1714.—this Reign was celebrated by the Victories by Land & Sea, of Marlborough, and Rooke.

Queen Anne was victorious by land and sea.

GEORGE 1.ST the first of the House of Brunswick Lunenburgh
from 1714 to 1727.—he landed at Greenwich 18.th September 1714.

And King George the First did with glory sway;

GEORGE 2.d from 1727 to 1760.— he was an able and courageous General and a good King.

But as King George the Second has long been dead.

GEORGE 3.ʳᵈ from 1760 who has ever set an example
of Virtue and Piety.

Long life to the George that we have in his stead.

GEORGE PRINCE of WALES, Regent from Feby 5.1811.
born Augst 12th 1762.

And may his son's son's to the end of the Chapter,
All come to be Kings in their turn.